CYN
(E14)
June 05

10321372

D0260536

'VERSI'

SP 418.00712
JON

Other titles in the series

CILT, the National Centre for Languages, seeks to support and develop multilingualism and intercultural competence among all sectors of the population in the UK.

CILT serves education, business and the wider community with:
- specialised and impartial information services;
- high quality advice and professional development;
- expert support for innovation and development;
- quality improvement in language skills and service provision.

CILT is a charitable trust, supported by the DfES and other Government departments throughout the UK.

NEW PATHFINDER

4

It makes you think!

Creating engagement, offering challenge

BARRY JONES &
ANN SWARBRICK

The views expressed in this publication are the authors' and do not necessarily represent those of CILT.

Acknowledgements

When ideas have come from named individuals we have acknowledged these in the text. We are particularly indebted to various groups of students and trainee teachers who have developed some of the suggestions in the book from humble beginnings and transformed them into challenging and inspired activities. These groups are or were based at St Martin's College, Lancaster; Homerton College, University of Cambridge; and CILT Graduate Teacher Programme. Without their often original thinking and practice we could not have written the book. Thanks to Antonio Lagocasal, Cynthia Geese and Xavier Martin for help with translations.

First published 2004 by CILT, the National Centre for Languages, 20 Bedfordbury, London WC2N 4LB

Copyright © CILT 2004, the National Centre for Languages 2004

ISBN 1 904243 34 7

A catalogue record for this book is available from the British Library

Photocopiable pages (60–61): the purchase of this copyright material confers the right on the purchasing institution to photocopy <the activity/resource pages> for their own use or for their students' use within the purchasing institution without any specific authorisation by the publisher. No other part of this publication may be reproduced, stored in a retrieval system, or transmitted in any form or by any means, electronic, mechanical, photocopying, recording or otherwise without prior permission in writing from CILT or under licence from the Copyright Licensing Agency Limited, of 90 Tottenham Court Road, London W1T 4LP.

The right of Barry Jones and Ann Swarbrick to be identified as authors of this work has been asserted by them in accordance with the Copyright, Designs and Patents Act, 1988.

Illustrations (pp17, 19 and 29) by Richard Duszczak
Printed in Great Britain by Hobbs

CILT Publications are available from: **Central Books**, 99 Wallis Rd, London E9 5LN. Tel: 0845 458 9910. Fax: 0845 458 9912. Book trade representation (UK and Ireland): **Broadcast Book Services**, Charter House, 29a London Rd, Croydon CR0 2RE. Tel: 020 8681 8949. Fax: 020 8688 0615.

contents

Introduction

Inspired by an INSET session on developing thinking skills in Geography, we decided to try and explore whether such ideas could work in MFL or whether we could at least put together a set of ideas which teachers could try out. We found at this INSET session that if we analysed many common-place activities in MFL the pupils were often not required to think very much. We began by taking some common activities and seeing if, by making slight alterations, we could transform them into more challenging tasks. This book is the result of our deliberations. We have tried to address the issue of status in our subject too since pupils sometimes perceive the learning that they do in MFL to be either babyish or unchallenging. Some also think that what they may have to say is not worth knowing. They may also believe that learning a language is a gargantuan task and that expertise is not within their grasp.

In research into boys' performance (Jones and Jones 2001) pupils were interviewed about their MFL experience. This is what two of them said:

> *'In other subjects they give you a topic ... tell you the facts and you learn them ... in languages you learn loads of vocabulary or you learn lots of sentences and questions.'*
>
> *'I think the girls are better at French. It's nothing to do with how their brain works, it's to do with boys just being boys. I don't think they concentrate as easy as girls and girls get down and get on with their work – sometimes I do try and sometimes I just can't be bothered ...'*

What is it about languages? Although the latter quotation could be a reflection on any subject, not just French, it may be time to take a fresh look at what and how we teach in MFL and to consider whether we always offer the kind of challenge that learners expect in a world in which they are bombarded with stimuli.

In England over the past few years, teachers have been presented with a centralised 'Key Stage 3 Strategy' in the Government's attempt to 'transform teaching and learning' at Key Stage 3 (ages 11–14). In this initiative one focus is on developing thinking skills. These have been defined elsewhere as:

- information processing;
- reasoning;
- enquiry;
- creative thinking;
- evaluation.

(DfEE/QCA 1999)

As teacher trainers with an obligation to discuss, explore and try out what this means in practice, we have involved our PGCE and GTP students and trainee teachers. This has enabled us to start with sound principles and practice developed over many years in our work with teachers in a large number of schools. In our writing we used McGuinness's helpful list of thinking strategies to stimulate our own ideas. These include, within the context of MFL classrooms:

1 Collecting information.
2 Sorting and analysing information.
3 Drawing conclusions.
4 Brainstorming new ideas.
5 Problem solving.
6 Determining cause and effect.
7 Evaluating options.
8 Planning and setting goals.
9 Decision making.
10 Reflecting upon one's own progress.

(McGuinness 1999)

We have incorporated all of these aspects somewhere in the book in an attempt to make you think!

Talk creates thought

- [ ] How significant is teacher and pupils' use of the target language in getting pupils thinking?

- [ ] What routines might we develop to ensure progression in the use of the target language?

- [ ] Which parts of the lesson are predictable and how can we exploit these occasions to develop pupils' expectations that they will communicate in the target language at those times?

chapter 1

As MFL teachers we have attempted over the past decade to maximise our use of target language in the classroom in an attempt to encourage pupils to do the same. This has sometimes been an uphill struggle, especially with older learners, but achieved with considerable success by some teachers. Work with student teachers on this aspect of teaching and learning has made us realise that, though it is fairly straightforward to reach a point where pupils accept the expectation that they will ask certain permissions in the language they are learning: Can I open the window? Can I take my jacket off?, etc, their use of target language sometimes doesn't go further than this. In addition, these phrases are not developed linguistically. So though the pupils may be interacting with the teacher in certain respects, they are far from talking to each other in the target language, since to do this in another language certainly takes much more thought than operating in English. What makes pupils think in the MFL classroom is an aspect which we cannot ignore.

The key is in the routine

The need to grapple for words in French, German or Spanish to put across a message is one of the thinking challenges which is missing for many pupils. It is not easy to engender a classroom culture in which searching for ways of expressing oneself is the expected norm. The key for us is in the routines we develop which set the expectation that pupils will use the target language. These will enable pupils to operate in the classroom with the language we model. Such language needs to be taught in the same way as any other linguistic content.

In this section we suggest some strategies which have been developed by our own trainee teachers for developing the use of target language during routine sections of the lesson. It is the experience of many of them that once the habit is established pupils are often drawn into the 'language learning game' which allows them the suspension of disbelief required to see the languages classroom as a non-English speaking area of the school. (We have also worked closely with James Burch and trainees and staff from St Martin's College, Lancaster over the years and would like to acknowledge their influence and inspiration on our work in this field.)

We will outline some strategies to demonstrate that an approach which is consistent and persistent can begin to pay dividends in terms of getting pupils to think. If this happens early on in pupils' language learning experience then using the target language becomes the norm rather than the exception.

Setting up classroom routines

We have come to understand the importance of routines in the MFL classroom. Though classrooms are complex places for the trainee teacher, for the experienced teacher there is much that is utterly predictable. It is this predictability which we are suggesting we profit from in terms of pupil learning. Think about everyday life in the classroom. There is a finite set of utterances that we routinely use during different parts of the lesson – the beginning, the objectives setting, the distribution of books, the setting up and implementation of pairwork activities, the rounding up of the lesson. We can predict what is likely to happen at these points with all but the most volatile of classes. These staging posts are potentially rich in language since this is the time when pupils may want to ask questions of you or talk to their partner. What we need to consider is how to channel pupils' energy into operating in the target language during these habitual moments. These routines can be used to develop pupils' use of the language and need to progress in line with the grammatical agenda we might have; the language needs to become more and more complex as pupils move through the year.

Let's look in detail at a scene where a class comes into the room, described on the following page. Here the teacher has picked up a phrase which he considers he'll be able to build on later – 'I did not hear. Could you repeat?' This example shows him specifically picking out that language for the class and drilling it.

Any newly emerging phrases such as the one above need drilling in the same way as you would drill a set of new nouns. To engage this class, in the example above, the teacher sets up conflict around the whereabouts of two of the pupils who have not arrived – are they skiving together? This becomes part of a real conversation though you can see that the teacher, James Stubbs, has in a sense set it up – i.e. he planned for it to happen. The interchange continues with other speculation about where Gareth is. The teacher sets in motion the language of speculation – probable/impossible, etc with the question *Qu'est-ce que tu penses?* The idea is to open up for them the possibility of speculating where someone could be and to give pupils the freedom to come up with their own suggestions.

T:	Gareth?	Gareth?
Class:	Absent.	Absent.
T:	Absent?	Absent?
Class:	Non.	No.
P:	Il sèche.	He's skiving.
T:	Il sèche? Gareth ... sèche? Non.	He's skiving? Gareth ... skiving? No.
Class:	Si!	Yes!
T:	Non!	No!
Class:	Si!	Yes!
Brian:	(words unclear)	
T:	Pardon? Allez-y la classe; on dit Brian ...	Pardon? Go on, class; we say Brian ...
Class:	Brian, je n'ai pas entendu.	Brian, I did not hear.
T:	Alors, je n'ai pas entendu. Toute la classe ...	So, I did not hear. Everyone ...
Class:	Je n'ai pas entendu ... veux-tu répéter, s'il te plaît.	I did not hear ... could you repeat please?
Brian:	Gareth est avec Janine.	Gareth is with Janine.
T:	Gareth et Janine, ils sèchent ... ensemble? Non!	Gareth and Janine, they are skiving ... together? No!
Class:	Si!	Yes!
T:	Non!	No!
Class:	Si!	Yes!

■ Commentary

What is happening?

Within the general discussion of who is absent and why, a familiar contradiction routine swings into action about whether Gareth is skiving or not. Although at an early stage in their learning, pupils are given the opportunity to provide their own explanations and to disagree with the teacher. Brian bravely leaps to Gareth's defence, saying he is with Janine. He does this quite tentatively, however, thus prompting the teacher to exploit the use of a newly-emerging phrase *Je n'ai pas entendu*. This is linked automatically by the class to the phrase *Veux-tu répéter s'il te plaît* – a phrase that the class by now is using spontaneously without any teacher prompting.

What is the teacher's grammatical agenda?

There are several items here that are part of the teacher's on-going grammatical agenda. These are:

* past tense with *Je n'ai pas entendu* with mimes that stress the subject pronoun, the negative and the past participle of a *–re* verb.
* use of modals with *Veux-tu répéter, s'il te plaît,* with lots of stress on the second person singular aspect of *vouloir.*

from *Something to say? Promoting spontaneous classroom language* (Harris et al 2001)

You can see from this example that the teacher is considering what language will be transferable to and useful in other contexts – he focuses on what we'll call 'high-currency' language and gets pupils to use this. This is language which will recur and which he can progressively build on throughout the year. He is building here a progressive curriculum for language which pupils habitually use in the classroom. This is the key, it seems to us, to encouraging pupils' use of the target language when they are talking either to the teacher or to their peers. As we have suggested, all too often this aspect of language goes no further than pupils asking permission of the teacher. And yet it requires real creative thought from pupils to sustain target-language use. As we have said, this type of **operational** language needs to be taught in the same way as any other element of language – it requires time within lessons, particularly in Year 7.

Let's explore some examples. Where in the lesson can we predict the possible dialogues – the language – pupils will want to use in order to operate in the target language? Where might this 'high-currency' language arise?

We've chosen three particular moments which are likely to recur lesson-on-lesson and have constructed a typical very short dialogue for each:

1   The beginning when you're finding out who is absent – the timed register.

2   The beginning when you're giving them the big picture of the lesson – setting objectives routine.

3   When pupils are doing a pair activity – dialogue around turn-taking.

1 The timed register

The timed register idea was developed by St Martin's College PGCE team. It's based on the idea that every moment counts in the language lesson and that routine moments can give rise to lots of language and are therefore worth making time for in the early days of learning a language. This is the sort of language which might arise from the situation in which the class tries to beat their last best time for taking the register. The teacher begins in the first couple of lessons but quickly pupils take over the role of register-taker. The idea can only work if pupils learn the 'register-taking' language. Here's how it might look over a series of lessons.

2 September, lesson 1
- Start teaching register routine
- Teach: *présent/absent* with mimes (bow = *présent*, cross arms = *absent* – need variations for gender markers)

4 September, lesson 2
- Reinforce *présent/absent* routine from lesson 1
- Receptive language: Let's time the register – Here's the stop watch – Who wants to time it? – Stop! – That took X seconds.
- Teach: Can I time it?

8 September, lesson 3
- Reinforce *présent/absent* routine
- Reinforce: Can I time it?
- Teach: That took X seconds.
- Teach numbers 1–10 and then tens to 60 (if not already learnt)
- Receptive language as for lesson 2: Let's time the register – Here's the stop watch – Who wants to time it? – Stop!

9 September, lesson 4
- Receptive language: Who wants to time it?
- Teach: Can I do it?
- Teach: Ready. Steady. Go ... Finished!
- Receptive language: How many seconds did it take?

11 September, lesson 5
- Repeat routine of lesson 4
- Begin recording on OHT chart

nom	*date*	*secondes*	*c'était comment?*
Damian	11 septembre	72	c'était lent

2 Setting objectives routine

There are a variety of ways in which you can make it clear to pupils what they will be learning in your lesson. We'll look at one particular routine you might like to adopt with your Year 7 or 8. This is based on an activity at the beginning of the lesson in which pupils from time to time predict what they will be learning in the lesson. (Our thanks to the St Martin's College MFL PGCE cohorts of 2002 and 2003 for showing us this idea in action.)

Here are some possible useful verbs pupils may want to use:

Dans cette leçon, on va/nous allons ... /In dieser Stunde werden wir ... /En esta lección vamos a ...

French	German	Spanish
décrire	etwas beschreiben	describir
trouver	etwas herausfinden	descubrir
dire	etwas sagen	decir
raconter	etwas erzählen	contar/decir
demander	etwas fragen	preguntar
apprendre	etwas lernen	aprender
savoir/connaître	etwas wissen	conocer
comprendre	etwas verstehen	entender
développer	etwas entwickeln	desarrollar
reconnaître	etwas erkennen	reconocer
mémoriser	etwas (auswendig) lernen	memorizar
utiliser	etwas benutzen	usar

Begin by teaching pupils selections of these verbs linked to a structure such as 'We are going to ...'. On the next page is a spinning top idea from Ruth Bailey, formerly of Alexandra Park School, for practising this language (it can be adapted for any new language).

In each of the sections of the spinning top you write some possible learning objectives for that lesson. Let's assume that you want to practise some of the verbs we have just looked at above and that your class are going to predict what you'll be doing in the lesson. As they enter, the spinning tops are on desks – one per pair of pupils. (We suggest, if available, using willing tutor group members to make the

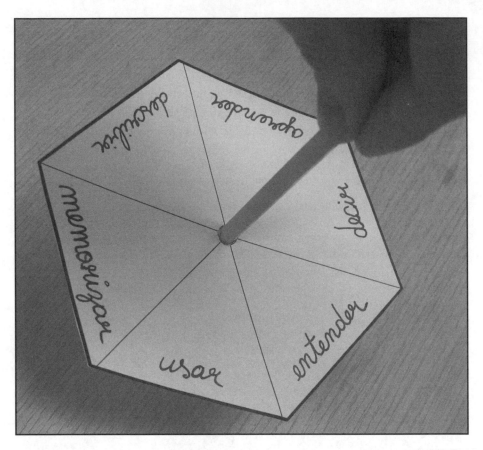

spinning tops in advance of the lesson.) The dialogue below is on the OHT, board or screen as pupils enter. One spins the top. The other has to embed the verb the spinning top falls on, into the dialogue. It will take two or more goes to get enough verbs to fill the blanks in the dialogue. In this way, they begin to practise in pairs, for approximately three minutes, the conversation they will have in the whole-class part of the lesson during which you'll reveal the actual objectives for that lesson. Their task is to guess as many of your objectives as possible.

On the next page is the dialogue to teach your pupils:

French	German	Spanish
A D'accord, qu'est-ce qu'on va/nous allons faire aujourd'hui?	A Also gut, was machen wir heute?	A Bien, ¿qué vamos a hacer hoy?
B Je pense qu'on va/nous allons ... (apprendre, lire, écrire, etc.)	B Ich denke/glaube wir werden ... (lernen, lesen, schreiben, usw.)	B Creo que vamos a ... (aprender, leer, escribir, etc.)
A Je suis d'accord./Je ne suis pas d'accord.	A Ich glaube/denke das auch./ Ich glaube/denke das nicht.	A Estoy de acuerdo./ No estoy de acuerdo.
B Et je pense qu'on va/ nous allons ...	B Und ich denke/glaube wir werden ...	B Y creo que vamos a ...
A Je pense qu'on va/ nous allons ...	A Ich glaube, wir werden ...	A Creo que vamos a ...
B Vérifions.	B Lass es uns herausfinden.	B Veamos.

Once pupils have had three minutes with the spinning tops, practising the dialogue, you then bring the whole class together and use the language from this model to discuss with them the objectives for the lesson. As a one-off this would be a waste of time but if you repeat the activity, say, twice per half term from the beginning of Year 7, pupils will pick up the routine. Plainly, such language can be useful in a range of different contexts. The expectation must be that during this activity the class will talk only in the target language, be that to each other or to you. Some teachers appoint a pupil observer to keep the class on task. We would need to consider, of course, whether this would be appropriate for any given class but if pupils take it in turns to be observer then it could be seen as a sort of privilege.

3 Dialogue around turn-taking

Setting up pairwork activities has become part and parcel of a language learning lesson. It is one way of making sure that all pupils engage in language practice, not just those who volunteer to answer the teacher's questions. It also enables them to work at their own pace. Pairwork is then another predictable moment in the lesson around which we could teach pupils the language they need to operate in the target language. Here's a possible dialogue to teach around a card game such as pelmanism – matching pictures to words:

French	German	Spanish
A *D'accord, tu commences.*	A *Also gut, du beginnst.*	A *Venga, tú empiezas.*
B *Non, tu commences.*	B *Nein, du beginnst.*	B *No, empiezas tú.*
A *D'accord ... à toi maintenant.*	A *Gut, du bist jetzt dran.*	A *Vale, ahora tú.*
B *C'est bon pour moi.*	B *Prima, jetzt ich.*	B *Vale, ahora yo.*
A *A ton tour.*	A *Du bist dran.*	A *Tu turno.*
B *Madame/Monsieur, on a fini/nous avons fini.*	B *Frau .../Herr ..., wir sind fertig.*	B *Señorita/Señora/Señor, hemos acabado.*

The dialogue will need modelling and drilling in the first instance. Here are some choral repetition ideas for use with such dialogues:

Chef d'orchestre

Divide the class notionally into two – one side taking the part of A and the other B. As you point to side A (like a conductor of an orchestra) they repeat the first line repeatedly until you point to the B section. Your baton stroke can dictate the speed at which you want the statement to be repeated. Young pupils tend to appreciate rapid variations in speed, skipping from very slow to very fast. This also works well if you notionally divide the class into four sections. (Pupil volunteers can also take the part of the conductor once the idea is established.) This is useful for drilling parts of sentences when pupils have pronunciation difficulties.

The 60-second challenge

Pupils repeat after you the first line of the dialogue several times at varying speeds until you are sure that the pronunciation is improving. The challenge is for the class to repeat the line (around the class, in turns, one by one) as many times as possible in 60 seconds. You or a pupil volunteer record the time it takes. The aim is to increase the number of repetitions they achieve in 60 seconds as they take on each new line of the dialogue. Once they have drilled the dialogue they are ready to return to your pairwork activity but you insist that pairs work in the target language using the dialogue they have just drilled. (This idea is from Jack Hunt School MFL department. Thanks to Yannick Crespy for it passing on to us.)

Thinking through routines

Many of us are at a disadvantage in that, unlike countries such as Sweden and Denmark, our classes change year on year. This means that continuity in the language used in routines needs to be common across a whole department for maximum effect. This is not always possible but it is useful with colleagues to think through and log, as departmental practice, the possible language to be taught around a particular routine. The Foreign Language Assistant (FLA) can also be useful here. To develop the turn-taking routine, etc, we observed and noted verbatim the language that two native speakers used while engaged in a pairwork activity. This could be something to do with native-speaker colleagues or FLAs. Consider constructing, for example, a bank of common dialogues around the following routine occurrences:

- Dialogue for giving excuses for lateness or absence – I'm sorry I'm late but ... I do apologise ... I'm terribly sorry ... ;

- Contradiction routines – Are you sure? Yes ... I think so/No I'm not sure but ... ;

- The language of negotiation in a competition – Can I have a point? What for? For getting it right/That's worth two points/I got that right/He got that wrong;

- Routine for disagreeing with you, the teacher, and for disagreeing with each other – the language of conflict, with its associated gestures and intonation, can give rise to excellent imitation by pupils.

From our own observations we conclude that pupils who are pushed to try to use the target language are pushed to think. The key to this is **teacher persistence** and **high expectations**. The sense of satisfaction when pupils begin to speak to you in the target language cannot be matched. But this is one of our toughest challenges in MFL because it doesn't happen by osmosis. We need to be constantly looking for ways of teaching pupils the language that they need and that they want to use while with us in the classroom. Make this a priority with a class that you enjoy teaching and we think you'll be convinced of the merits of this way of working.

key points	• Using routines which encourage pupils' use of the target language can provide an element of challenge.
	• Perseverance and insistence on target language use is very demanding of pupils and it forces them to think.
	• Teaching pupils dialogues for predictable moments in the lesson gives them the tools they need to stay in the target language, but this language needs to be taught systematically.

Creating engagement, offering challenges

- [ ] How can we get pupils thinking as well as repeating as we present new language to them?

- [ ] How can we create time in busy lessons for pupils to think out and prepare their responses to our questions?

- [ ] Can working with a partner help pupils to think?

- [ ] What can be done at the start of the lesson to encourage real engagement with the language?

chapter 2

Presenting new language

When presenting new language to a group of learners common practice normally involves showing a picture or a series of pictures on the OHP screen, holding up objects or showing flashcards. We then ask the class to imitate and repeat aloud the sound of the new word. If the pupils have never met the language before this seems to be an efficient way of introducing them to unfamiliar sound combinations and encouraging accurate imitation. Within a few minutes, however, because the initial appeal of the activity diminishes, most learners need something more to sustain their motivation, especially if the teacher believes, probably correctly, that more choral or individual repetition is still required. At this stage in the lesson it may be helpful to invent and insert a modest challenge, a reason for thinking.

If we ask our pupils to make a decision whether something is pretty or ugly, good or less good for our health, old fashioned or 'cool' we are asking them to think. We can extend the example into a classifying task if we present them with a list of, say, clothes and ask them to put each item of clothing into either a column headed 'old fashioned' or one headed 'cool'. The categories we choose can vary according to topic but the format of the activity stays the same no matter what the context. It is this form of thinking skill which we will explore and which we believe can be used at the beginning of lessons to add additional interest and help sustain motivation, when repetition of the new language is nonetheless still required.

Here are a few commonly taught topics and the categories under which new vocabulary can be classified as it is being rehearsed. The first topic is 'where the pupils live'. The context is one in which a Year 7 class is preparing a description to include in an exchange of e-mails or fax messages with a French class.

La maison

Having presented items of furniture using pictures cut out of magazines the class can classify the furniture under headings:

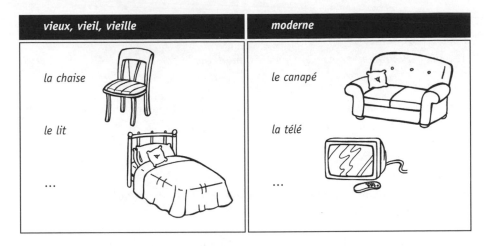

vieux, vieil, vieille	moderne
la chaise	le canapé
le lit	la télé
...	...

As the pupils are repeating the word the teacher displays the picture or the word in one of the two columns. To begin to model and establish **classroom interaction language** he or she can ask questions like:

- *Ici ou là?*
- *A droite ou à gauche?*
- *Vous êtes d'accord?*

To help set up a routine and as a memo to the teacher – as well as an aid for pupils who cannot always tell right from left – the words *à droite* and *à gauche* can be permanently displayed at the top of the whiteboard.

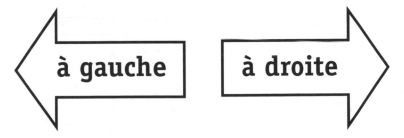

à gauche — à droite

When the learners are familiar with these questions the pupils' language can be **extended** by the teacher asking for a **reason** for each choice made. In French the interaction might be:

Teacher	*L'armoire … à droite ou à gauche?*
Pupil	*A droite.*
Teacher	*Pourquoi? C'est vieux ou c'est moderne?*
Pupil	*C'est moderne.*

A **further extension** for more able or more advanced classes might be to use the appropriate adjective to qualify the noun, for example:

Teacher	*L'armoire … à droite ou à gauche?*
Pupil	*A droite.*
Teacher	*Pourquoi? C'est une vieille armoire ou c'est une armoire moderne?*
Pupil	*C'est une armoire moderne.*

The language practice has the advantage, in language learning terms, of the teacher using the definite article in the first mention of the item of furniture and then the change to indefinite article in the follow-up questions. These models of a problematic grammatical feature, as well as the illustration of different forms of gender marker, should be the subject of class discussion. To help raise awareness of the grammatical patterns different colours (blue and red) can be used to show the difference between masculine and feminine nouns. If the words *le/la*, *un/une* are written on large, **movable** cards, these can be placed in the appropriate positions in different, already practised, sentences on the whiteboard. Pupils can then be asked in pairs to formulate a rule in English to explain the difference not only between the use of *un* and *une* but in one instance why *le* or *la* is used and why, in another, *un* or *une*. Thinking skills should be clearly in evidence in this activity, and, most importantly, the words used in the explanations are those of the learners rather than those of their teachers.

The prompts in this sequence might include:

La chaise?   *Et l'armoire?*
Et le canapé?   *Et la télé?*
Et la table?

In a follow-up sequence the indefinite article is used when an adjective is added:

C'est une vieille chaise?   *C'est un vieux lit?*
C'est un canapé moderne? *C'est une télé moderne?*
C'est une vieille table?

Other topics and related categories could include:

les vêtements	moche, moches	joli, jolis, jolie, jolies
le pull		nice pullover ☺
la cravate	horrible tie ☹	
la chemise	horrible shirt ☹	
le pantalon		
les chaussettes		
les chaussures		
la jupe		
les baskets		

Questions that can be asked in this example might be:

Teacher: *A droite ou à gauche?*
         Pourquoi?

And possible answers, always modelled first:

Parce que c'est vieux.   *Parce que c'est trop grand.*
Parce que c'est nouveau. *Parce que c'est trop petit …*

Other possible topics and categories are:

la nourriture	bon pour la santé	pas très bon pour la santé
les chips		
les tomates		
les salades		
le bifteck		
les croissants		
les hamburgers		
...		

les transports	rapide	lent, lente
le train		
la voiture		
l'avion		
la moto		
le bus		
la fusée		
le bateau		
le patin à roulettes		
...		

Que sais-je?

To extend the examples further, pupils can be challenged by tests of their general knowledge at the same time as their proficiency in the target language. For example, the teacher draws two columns, left-hand headed *récent*, right-hand headed *ancien*.

As a picture is shown of each of the inventions pupils imitate and repeat the word and add either *c'est récent* or *c'est ancien*. The teacher then puts the picture in the appropriate column.

les inventions	récent	ancien
la radio		
le DVD		
le magnétoscope		
le portable		
le micro-ondes		
le réveil		
le lecteur CD		
l'appareil photo		
la machine à laver		
l'horloge		
la boussole		
le jeu vidéo		
...		

Categories for classification

Contrasting categories in French might include some of those presented below. These are best chosen according to the topic being taught and to the language level of the learners. (From the list below, opinions about clothes, for example, might be used.) Many are appropriate in a number of different contexts so are worth practising. If modelled first by the teacher, pupils can use the language to justify their opinions or to give a reason why an item belongs in one category rather than in another. Other synonyms are, of course, possible!

riche	pauvre	amusant	sérieux
chaud	froid	dur	mou
tentant	pas tentant	rêveur	réaliste
régulier	irrégulier	bizarre	normal
travailleur	paresseux	surprenant	banal
confus	clair	optimiste	pessimiste
cher	pas cher	facile	difficile
cool	stressant	célèbre	inconnu
court	long	stupide	intelligent
agréable	désagréable	triste	heureux
délicieux	immonde	faible	fort
actif	inactif	attirant	répugnant
simple	compliqué	ravi	déçu
vrai	faux	épicé	fade
ennuyeux	intéressant		

Allowing time for thinking

Categorising activities is important for encouraging thinking. This is a dimension which we suggest adding to the familiar 'listen and repeat' choral or group imitation and repetition of language. There are times, however, when we want more complex responses from more able learners or when we need to give slower groups more support. In either case picking on individuals can sometimes challenge them too quickly and lead to embarrassment and a lack of self-esteem. We may not have given them sufficient time to think out what to say and also how to say it in the target language. Here are some strategies designed to help pupils by giving them a moment or two longer to think. To keep their confidence high the strategies are designed to encourage our learners to try out their response very quickly with a friend before either is asked to speak in public. In this way we take the heat off individuals and allow them time to work out what they are going to say and how to say it.

Practising, at the beginning of a lesson, language already met before:

1 Chuchotez! (Whispering pairs)

Instead of asking individuals to answer by themselves the teacher can have pairs of pupils first **whisper an answer** to each other. This is a very helpful strategy when asking learners to:

- recall previously learned vocabulary;
- respond to an instruction given in the target language;
- answer a 'why' question about some aspect of the language you are about to teach or have just taught.

Here are some ideas based on the whispering strategy. (With acknowledgement to Claire Ali for this idea.)

To help recall the teacher asks:

Qu'est-ce que c'est? (showing a small part of a picture on the OHP screen) and adds: *Chuchotez à vos partenaires!*

To clarify instructions the teacher gives the instruction:

Dessinez un monstre avec trois têtes, quatre jambes et deux bras and adds: *Qu'est-ce que vous devez faire? Décidez en anglais avec votre partenaire. Vous avez dix secondes.* [Waits, then asks:] *Alors, qu'est-ce que vous devez faire? En anglais …*

To formulate a grammatical rule. The teacher has just illustrated and taught the agreement of colour adjectives in French. He or she has added an *e* written on card in red to the adjective *vert* describing *une souris* and an *s* written on card in green to the adjective *jaune* describing *des perroquets*. The teacher says:

*Une souris verte. Pourquoi est-ce qu'il y a un **e** à la fin de 'verte'?*
*Des perroquets jaunes. Pourquoi est-ce qu'il y a un **s** à la fin de 'jaunes'?*
Décidez en anglais avec votre partenaire. Vous avez une minute.

Rationale for whispering pairs:

- All learners are involved.

- Every (or nearly every) person attempts to have an answer ready.
- Even if some individuals do not supply an answer all have been on task.
- If asked, one pupil can give his or her own answer or that of the partner.
- Personal embarrassment of not knowing an answer is avoided; a pair can say *'nous ne savons pas'*, thus sharing responsibility.
- The teacher can be asked (in examples 2 and 3) to check responses before these are made public.

2 Multipliez vos idées (Multiply your ideas)

Any brainstorming activity lends itself to *Multipliez vos idées*. This technique allows for pupil preparation and thought before the whole-class brainstorm. Here are some examples:

- *Ecrivez les noms de tous les animaux que nous avons mentionnés hier.*
- *Vous allez écouter une description de ma maison. Imaginez! Quels sont les mots que je vais mentionner? Ecrivez une liste.*

1 Individuals work to produce an initial list.
2 Each pupil then shares with someone else his or her list, correcting and/or adding new language as appropriate.
3 Pairs then share their joint list with another pair.
4 Each group of four then checks the enlarged list against one the teacher has prepared in advance and which is shown on the OHP or interactive whiteboard. Additions are made if appropriate. N.B. whole-class feedback takes too long and is infrequently engaging.

Rationale:

The language lists help pupils recall what has already been taught in a positive and collaborative way. Less able learners are helped by more able peers and learning is extended by each pupil in ways which are individual and non-judgemental. Everyone feels he or she has contributed to the list in some way.

Apprenez ensemble (Learn together)

Having presented in a previous lesson some new language – as exemplified in a topic such as food which we have just seen – begin a follow-up lesson with a paired 'spelling practice' activity. Each pupil has to help his or her partner either spell individual words accurately or write a limited number of sentences without spelling mistakes. Since there is a sequence of teacher actions we will present these suggestions as a series of stages.

Objective: paired spelling practice of foods, the names of which have already been thoroughly practised orally. In French this could look like this:

une omelette	*un œuf au plat*	*un jus d'orange*
un hotdog	*des chips*	*un yaourt*
du fromage	*de la limonade*	*un gâteau*
du pâté	*des bonbons*	*une banane*
un croque monsieur	*des biscuits*	*une pomme*

Setting up the activity The teacher gives to each pair of pupils one complete list of words where the spelling is being revised and one puzzle sheet; the puzzle sheet shows some words with one letter missing (e.g. *une om–lette*), some with a number of letters replaced by + (e.g. *de l+ l+mon+de*) some with just an initial letter and – – – – to show how many letters are needed in a correct version (e.g. *y – – – – –*), some with only the bottom half of the word showing (see p42 for an example); add a note like: *il y a deux accents â, un é et une lettre étrange œ.* Both pupils spend 60 seconds looking at the one complete list of words, then both:

1 attempt to complete the one puzzle sheet together, without reference to the complete list;
2 check their attempt against the correct spelling on the teacher's list;
3 decide on which approaches help them learn the correct spelling most efficiently; this strategy can then become a way to test themselves when they are given a homework designed to encourage accurate spelling.

It would be easy to add an element of challenge to the memorisation activity described in *Apprenez ensemble* above. The stages involved might be:

Stage 1

When the class has learnt the names of foods the teacher starts the example by putting some of the words remembered by the pupils into two columns, headed 'healthy living' – 'less healthy living'. This is a classifying task as exemplified earlier.

c'est bon pour la santé	c'est moins bon pour la santé
une pomme	des chips
…	…

As the teacher does this he or she begins to model the **language of agreement and disagreement** with the class. This can then be used later by pupils to help them respond to each other's suggestions:

Teacher   *Une pomme. C'est bon pour la santé, n'est-ce pas?*

Teacher   [responding to next word offered]
               Une banane. C'est bon pour la santé ou c'est moins bon pour la santé? John?

Teacher   [whispers to John] *C'est moins bon pour la santé ou c'est bon pour la santé?*

John   *C'est bon …*

Teacher   *La classe? Vous êtes tous d'accord?*
               Tracey, tu es d'accord? Peter, et toi? Tu es d'accord?
               Moi, je suis d'accord. Une banane. C'est bon pour la santé.
               Et les biscuits. C'est bon pour la santé ou c'est moins bon pour la santé?
               …

Stage 2

Teacher   *Travaillez à deux.*
               Donnez-moi le nom de deux choses à manger. [asks a pair to make a suggestion]

Pair   *Un gâteau.*
               Un jus d'orange.

Stage 3

Teacher writes *un gâteau* and *un jus d'orange* in the *'c'est moins bon pour la santé'* column.

Teacher   *Vous êtes d'accord? Un jus d'orange est bon pour la santé ou moins bon pour la santé? Et un gâteau? Tout le monde est d'accord?*
Mary et Jane, vous êtes d'accord? John, toi ausi? Tu es d'accord?
Moi, je ne suis pas d'accord. A mon avis, un jus d'orange est bon pour la santé. Mais un gâteau – je ne sais pas. C'est moins bon pour la santé, mais c'est délicieux!

and so on.

Other challenges at the start of a lesson

Lesson beginnings lend themselves to short activities which help the class start thinking in the language they are learning. These are best if they are revision of previously practised language. However since the word **revision** is not going to motivate classes who are expecting something a little more engaging – it is after all a new lesson – here are a few suggestions to try.

Cherchez l'intrus (Odd one out)

Display a text on the OHP. Ask the class to identify the odd one out. At a simple level this might be a word which is out of place in an otherwise homogenous group (*voiture, train, avion, ananas*). At a more advanced level this might be a sentence out of place within a short text along the lines of 'One beautiful grey summer's day Jean was very hot. He was wearing his shorts with his skis …'

When such an activity is introduced for the first time use odd one out where there is only one possible 'candidate'. However, in order to provoke discussion, a later stage might be to include more than one so that there can be class debate.

Anagrams

A quick way of engaging a class is to display on the whiteboard or OHP a number of anagrams of words recently taught. Pupils come into the classroom and have something immediate to do. Spelling is reinforced and if this activity is done individually, then in pairs, it can be checked quickly. If some do not finish it does not matter! An example from the list on p25 might be:

- pshci (*chips*)
- ourtay (*yaourt*)
- tooghd (*hotdog*)

Through the keyhole

Put a cut-out keyhole over part of a picture already used but which is not easily identifiable. Pupils have to guess in the target language – either in writing or orally – what the keyhole reveals.

Quick sentences

Write five familiar words on the whiteboard. The class is challenged to produce **as quickly as possible** (timed with a watch) five sentences each with one of the words correctly used in it. This can be done by individuals, pairs of pupils or by tables. *Bons points* can be awarded to individuals or to tables of pupils; if the latter strategy is adopted collaboration seems to increase motivation.

Expand your answer

Have permanently written in a corner of the whiteboard or on a wall display the words (for French) *et, mais, en plus, puis, aussi*. If in their answer to everyday questions asked at the beginning of a lesson the pupils extend a simple statement using one of these words they gain a *bon point*.

Examples:

Teacher   *Ça va?*
Pupil 1   *Oui, ça va bien **mais** Kirsty est malade.*
Pupil 2   *Oui, ça va bien **et en plus** il fait du soleil.*

Teacher	[seeing lunch sandwiches in pupil's bag]
	Tu aimes les sandwichs?
Pupil	*Oui, j'aime les sandwichs **mais** je préfère les chips!*
Teacher	*Tu as froid, Peter?*
Peter	*Oui, j'ai froid **et** il pleut …*

(Thanks to Katherine Richardson PGCE Key Stage 2/3 student and MFL teachers at Greneway (Middle) School, for this idea.)

Ça ne va pas! (That's not right!)

Display a text in which there are several illogical statements. Pairs have to identify these. Example:

Par un beau jour d'été à six heures du soir, Julien qui est fils unique, est allé en ville avec son frère, Michel. Le soleil brillait mais il faisait froid. 'J'aime bien l'hiver,' dit Michel. 'C'est ma saison préférée.' Ils sont partis à vélo et sont allés au marché pour rencontrer leurs amis. Juliette, une fille petite et grande, était déjà là. 'Si on allait au ciné?' dit-elle. Ils étaient tous d'accord. 'Mais, allons-y rapidement. Ça commence à quatre heures'. La pluie était affreuse mais une fois arrivés au théâtre ils étaient contents. La pièce était très bien jouée!

Bon journaliste, mauvais journaliste? (Are you a good reporter?)

Show a cartoon/photo and a written description of what is depicted. This should contain a few inaccuracies. The class has to identify what is incorrectly reported.

Again, the teacher should avoid saying what is incorrect. This is best coming from groups and being voted on, quickly, before the teacher intervenes.

C'est difficile ou c'est facile? (Easy or hard?)

Using a list of words from a previous lesson shown on the OHP, pupils in pairs either write a list of words they find difficult to pronounce, or say the words they find difficult to spell.

Looking at the list which one pupil finds hard to pronounce, the other pupil listens carefully to the teacher, tries to remember accurately what has been said, then spends a few seconds trying to help his or her partner improve. If spelling is a problem the same mutual help is given by one pupil to the other, using spelling games already described (see p10).

For other ideas for challenging beginnings see the Appendix.

key points	• **Presenting new language through flashcards can be more than a repetition exercise.** • **Having to classify language requires thought from pupils.** • **Pupils need time to think in MFL lessons.** • **Rehearsing responses with a partner before sharing them with the class builds confidence.**

It makes you think ...

- [ ] What is the purpose of the questions we ask regularly in MFL lessons?

- [ ] What types of questions require pupils to think before they reply?

- [ ] Do questions that focus on content always reveal depth of understanding?

- [ ] Should questions always be asked in the target language?

chapter 3

The previous two chapters have been substantially about aiming to build up and to model systematically the 'non topic specific' target language which we want learners to use with their teacher and with each other, and encouraging them to respond in reflective ways to the language we present in class. Our aim throughout is to encourage thinking rather than an ability to reproduce a set response or to repeat verbatim the language. What is important is the relationship between what pupils do and whether it makes them think. If what they do does not make them think our intention is not necessarily to abandon certain practices but to identify what is needed in order to transform the activity and add challenge.

Responses made by learners are often, although not exclusively, the result of questions we ask in class. Some kinds of questions are challenging and make learners struggle to come up with a response. Other questions make few or even no demands, either linguistic or cognitive, on pupils in our classrooms. This chapter will explore what makes a difference, what makes you think.

If we think of the **outcome** of questioning we can come up with a list which includes:

1 recalling facts;
2 producing an explanation;
3 giving a reason;
4 making a comparison.

To produce these outcomes different questions are needed which either decrease or increase cognitive challenge. On the one hand factual recall can be a response to a closed question and offer minimal challenge. Producing an explanation, on the other hand, is normally the response to an open question and nearly always offers a greater challenge.

Let's test this out. Here is a sample of random questions recorded verbatim in a number of classrooms by secondary PGCE students in Cambridge. The year group involved is shown by a number after the question. The number in Roman numerals is the set: i = top set, ii = second set, etc; b = bottom; m/a is mixed ability.

Consider what kind of response each question requires. What word(s), if any, does the teacher expect the class to say? Which questions require just a yes/no answer? Which questions can be answered very simply yet lend themselves to being extended by a supplementary question to challenge the learners? Which questions are, in themselves, linguistically demanding? Which make the class think and which merely require recall of previously encountered language? Are there some questions you would not use in a language lesson? Explain exactly what you believe the classes' responses could or should be. Then try the activity which we suggest below.

1	*Stuart est ici aujourd'hui?* 10i
2	*Peux-tu décrire ta maison?*10i
3	*Tu as ta propre chambre?* 10i
4	*Alice, tu veux finir la phrase?* 10i
5	Does everyone think that the sentence is correct? 10i
6	What rules do you know about adjectives? 10i
7	*Le onze septembre*; what am I saying, Marie? 7m/a
8	*Film première*; what does it mean? 7m/a
9	*Qu'est-ce qui manque?* 7m/a
10	*Qu'est-ce que vous voyez?* 7m/a
11	*C'est numéro deux?* 7m/a
12	*Qu'est-ce qu'on peut rajouter pour améliorer la phrase?* 9i
13	Have you got a problem at the back? 9i
14	*Qu'est-ce que tu as dit?* 9i
15	How would you say 'she plays tennis'? 9i
16	*Qu'est-ce que vous avez fait le weekend?* 8ii
17	*Quelle est la capitale de la Belgique?* 8ii
18	*Qui peut l'aider?* 8ii
19	What's the difference between *'habt ihr'* and *'hast du'*? 9i
20	What other way could you ask a question instead of using *'hast du'*? 9i
21	*Habt ihr ein Haus oder eine Wohnung?* 9i
22	What is a way of getting good marks? 9i (expected reply: 'expressing an opinion')
23	Did you manage to do that Nicole? 9i
24	What did we do last lesson? 9i
25	What did I say you'd be doing this lesson? 9i
26	How many examples of past tense are there? 9i
27	*Was würdest du sagen, Stephanie ... für B?* 9i
28	How did you work that out? 9i
29	*Kannst du Ski fahren? Richtig oder falsch?* 9i
30	*Noch etwas?* 9i
31	Past participles ... what have you learnt about them? 9i
32	*Sono contenti? Perché?* 8b
33	*Quali animali ci sono nella foto?* Is it a dog? 8b
34	*Gary, hai una serpente? O un pappagallo? Parla? Non? È stupido?* 8b
35	*Come si chiama questo negocio? Che cosa vendono qui?* 8b

36	What's the imperfect tense? 10i
37	What's the ending for *'nous'*? 10i
38	What are you confused about? 10i
39	That's not a good start, is it? 9i
40	*Souvent?* 9i
41	Can I hear someone talking? 9i
42	Can anyone offer a suggestion? 9i
43	*Comment t'appelles-tu?* (six times) 8b
44	Why are you late? 8b
45	*Où habites-tu?* (five times) 8b
46	Michael, what did Nicola say? 8b
47	*Qu'est-ce que c'est 'un collège'?* 8iv
48	Is *'mon copain'* a male or a female friend? 8iv
49	*¿Qué es esto?* 7m/a
50	How would you say 'I have a pencil case'? 7m/a
51	*Rachel, tu es là?* 8ii
52	*Tu vas mieux? Ça va maintenant?* 8ii
53	*Où est Matthew?* 8ii
54	Did anyone get less than 5? 8ii
55	*'Puis'* means 'then', doesn't it? 8ii
56	Why don't you pronounce *'ent'*? 9i
57	*Tout est clair?* 9i
58	*Tu es en train de manger quelque chose?* 9i
59	*Tu crois?* 9i
60	*Vous voyez tous le tableau?* 9i

Here is a sorting task. Categorise the questions above into one of these three columns.

No challenge	Low challenge	High challenge
E.g. *Comment tu t'appelles, Peter?*	E.g. *C'est un éléphant ou c'est un lion?*	E.g. *Tu aimes le chocolat. Pourquoi?*

In the example here the low-challenge question (*C'est un éléphant ou c'est un lion?*) has a legitimate place because its focus is most likely on recall and correct pronunciation. However, does it make you think? Do we shy away from high-challenge questions because they are difficult to construct in languages? Are there ways to transform low-challenge questions into ones which make greater cognitive demands?

Let's take some of the examples from the list above and consider what needs to be done. Invariably the addition of a follow-up question makes a greater demand on the learner. For example, with young learners, in the context of using hidden flashcards, we can question pupils' certainty about the answer they have given, like this:

Teacher   *C'est un éléphant ou c'est un lion?*
Pupil   *C'est un lion:*
Teacher   *Tu es certain?*
Pupil   *Euh ... Oui.*

[Teacher reveals card]

Teacher   *Voilà! Tu as raison!*

In this example the question, *'Tu es certain?'* introduces an element of doubt and, for more advanced learners, offers the possibility to negotiate. Without an extension of the question there is a danger that the pupils will not be thinking. How can we make it more challenging?

Let's explore in more detail what the sequence in questioning might be. The pattern is usually that, as a first step, the teacher asks a question to which the answer is yes or no. For example, in French:

Teacher   [showing a picture of a rhinoceros] *C'est un rhinocéros, oui ou non?*
Pupil   *Oui!*

The next step is to ask a question where the correct response is the last word in the teacher's choice of alternatives. For example:

Teacher   *C'est un éléphant ou c'est un lion?*
Pupil   *C'est un lion!*

The third and last step is an open-ended question:

Teacher [showing a photograph] *Qu'est-ce que c'est?*

In elementary stages of teaching a foreign language the practice of three-stage questioning seems entirely legitimate because the learners need to be supported. However, after the early stages the learners quickly recognise the game and cease to think about the answer. They are sophisticated enough to realise that the teacher is in effect feeding them the right answer so what's the point of thinking? The mechanical nature of the technique takes over and learners cease to focus on meaning. They are being cooperative and, in their minds, in a sense, **allowing** us to teach without putting in any great effort to learn. A good example of learners accepting being spoon fed. An easy life!

In addition to provoking thought an additional question not only makes the pupil think but can begin the practice of a sequence of synonyms or alternatives such as *'(Tu es) sûr'? 'Vraiment'?*, etc which can be set in train over time. The use of these supplementary questions is even more legitimate if there is a genuine reason for some doubt, when for example, only part of the projected image or photo is visible, or a keyhole mask only allows part of the scene to be visible, or if a word is projected as a mirror image and upside down on the screen! If carefully planned, a teacher's questioning can encourage learners to use *'(je suis) certain'*, *'(je ne suis) pas certain'* and other words with similar meanings in their own responses at a later date.

Types of question

Since question and answer constitute much of the interaction we have with pupils it makes sense to take a closer look at what we are expecting from this process. Let's consider in more detail the types of questions we ask in MFL classrooms. As we have seen from the sorting task above, some questions are directed at the content of the lesson and others at the language itself – often arising from grammatical patterns.

Focus on content

If we look at the list of 60 questions collected at random, the most common question types are:

a Questions which ask for information: accretion

These questions require the learner to recall facts or recognise previously learnt language. They are closed questions which seek a single correct answer.

C'est quel sport? (looking at a partly hidden picture)
Que fait X?
C'est quoi en français? (looking at a whole picture)

b Questions which call for reflection: judgemental

These questions provide personal answers. They involve giving an opinion.

Pourquoi X, est-il mieux pour la santé que Y?
Pourquoi préfères-tu habiter en ville ou à la campagne?

Focus on understanding

We are very familiar with question types **a** and **b** above. It is less frequent in teaching MFL to think about questions which really focus on pupils' understanding of the language. This may be because, in our eagerness to maximise our use of the target language, those questions which do elicit understanding may require too complex a command of the language for pupils to be able to express themselves except at the most advanced levels. And yet the answers to these tell us most about how pupils are progressing beyond simple recall of facts or known vocabulary. Let's consider the types of questions which pupils are asked for instance in History. These questions are designed to elicit understanding as opposed to information and it is these types of question which make pupils think hardest and bring into play the skills they are developing as emergent historians. These could be subdivided into two types of question:

a Questions which allow for more than one right answer: divergent

These questions demand imaginative thinking and the ability to solve problems. In History these might include:

• How could the design of this project be improved?
• Looking at a collection of items, what interpretations of these events can you suggest?

b Questions which seek the most appropriate or best answer: convergent

These questions focus on what is already known. They might require explanations or comparisons. In History these might include:

- Why was this letter written?
- Does the evidence suggest that it is right to suppose that … ?

What happens in our own classroom situations? If divergent and convergent questions get to the crux of understanding are there times when we need systematically to devise them for our own MFL learners? We might think of a line of progression for the questions we ask going from those which elicit information to those which elicit understanding. If so there may be a point when use of English is appropriate depending on the complexity of the answers we require. In terms of demanding thought from pupils, better at some point to ask the questions which get to the heart of the matter, even if in English, than to stick to simple word recognition or information retrieval.

Let's look at divergent questions first.

An example of a divergent question in MFL might be, at the end of a topic on holidays to Mauritius:

- *Le tourisme, est-il efficace pour la Maurice?* (Is tourism good for Mauritius?)

Here pupils are being offered the possibility of looking beyond the holiday brochures to consider the impact of tourism on indigenous people.

Another example of a divergent question:

- How do you ask someone's name in French?

Here you're allowing pupils to see that when people ask their name it could come in a variety of forms: *Comment t'appelles-tu? Tu t'appelles comment? Tu es? Qui es-tu?*

Now let's consider convergent questions.

An example of a convergent question in MFL might be, in a topic on healthy eating:

- Why is menu X more balanced than menu Y?

This could be tackled with simple structures in the target language:

- X is more balanced because it has ... and this is good for energy.
- There are X calories in ...

Another example of a convergent question in MFL:

- Here are the different parts of the verb *'être'*. We call it an 'irregular' verb. From this example, can you explain what an irregular verb is?

This could be very challenging for a pupil in Year 8 or 9 to answer in the target language and yet this is a vital stage in linguistic development – beginning to see that established patterns can be broken. A good explanation of this by a pupil in English is useful and necessary evidence of progression in linguistic development.

Preventing disengagement; maintaining interaction

Picture this

It's Year 8. You're half way through the lesson. You've been teaching the names of different sporting activities in French. You've taught orally five sports for which the verb *'faire'* is appropriate and five for which *'jouer'* is required. So far things have been going well. The class has been telling you orally what sports they play. Pronunciation has been good and most of the group – the boys as well as the girls – are keen to speak about their sporting activities. Now you judge it's the right time for you to pull the strands together and to reveal the grammatical pattern. As planned, you decide to write up the list of sports in two columns, one headed *'faire ...'* and the other *'jouer ...'* You turn your back and start to write on the whiteboard. Then the murmur starts. They've switched off. However, you've no choice but to continue; before they can do the writing activity that you've planned – writing a description of the sports they play – they need the list on the board. Normally you would perhaps have prepared a list on the OHP or interactive whiteboard precisely to avoid the 'switch off' factor. But today there was just not enough time ...

How is it that, the moment you start writing, pupils, more often than not, leave you, the teacher, to get on with it? Is it because, until you've **finished** the writing, it is not going to be their turn? Or is it because there is no interest for pupils in the **process** of **you** writing the words on the board? Both reasons are perhaps true. In a sense you've taken possession of what's happening for as long as it takes you to write the French, and for many this can seem an age. The result is likely to be relative or complete disengagement, unless it's a class predisposed to unquestioning willingness. Look at it from their point of view; there is nothing for them to **do** while you are writing. Nothing links them intrinsically to the thought processes you're going through as you transfer the words from your head to the board. No doubt you have solutions but for our student teachers this is a problem. How do you keep pupils engaged and thinking?

Suggestion 1
Stop mid-word, turn to the class and ask them to complete the last few letters of the word you are in the process of writing. For example, if you are writing a cognate and you have got as far as *'footb…'* it should not be difficult for pupils to complete this word even if they have not seen it written in French before. This process may be helped along with less obvious spellings if you say the words before asking the class to complete them.

Example:

'Je fais de l'équitation' could stop after *'équi…'* because the combination of letters in *'tation'* is exactly the same in other words they have already encountered such as *'natation'*. This also helps reinforce sound/writing/spelling relationships.

Suggestion 2
Stop mid-sentence and ask the pupils to predict what comes next. This could be raising grammatical awareness, making a distinction between *'faire du …'* and *'jouer au …'* (+ name of sport), both of which you and they have rehearsed orally previously. Alternatively you could stop before the name of the sport and invite guesses.

Suggestion 3
You say something which is obviously incorrect and wait, without comment, for the pupils to notice your deliberate mistake.

Suggestion 4
You hesitate over the spelling of a word as if you've forgotten how to spell it.

Suggestion 5
Half way through a word, again without any kind of comment, you pass the board pen to one of the pupils to complete what you have started.

As well as keeping the learners' attention focused where you want it these strategies help classroom management. As one of the findings in the CILT/QCA publication, *Boys' performance in MFL* (Jones and Jones 2001) summarises:

> *[In order to maintain attention] boys respond positively to explanations when these are interactive [...]. Some pupils showed concern that, when the main objective in a lesson was to explain a particular language point, teachers did not always adopt a dialogic or interactive approach. Pupils often perceived this approach as being insensitive to their pedagogic needs. In turn, this may compromise the learning that takes place.* (p23)

A missing dimension: accurate copying

Copying accurately is a skill which presents problems for all but the most able learners. In order that pupils' spelling does not let them down we focus here on ways in which accurate spelling can be developed systematically. We suggest a number of different techniques so that, as far as possible, variety ensures motivation, especially since this is clearly an activity which requires concentration and attention to detail. Every suggestion encourages learners to look at individual words and words in appropriate contexts, in order to spell them aloud. As a given we are assuming that to do this pupils use the alphabet of the language they are learning, and that the vocabulary has been thoroughly practised orally beforehand. The focus is on letter-by-letter and letter combinations – and learners definitely have to think!

Having written up or displayed a word or words (this works best on the whiteboard or on the OHP) the teacher can:

- mask the bottom half of the word(s) displayed; pupils spell aloud using the target-language alphabet;

un

h~m~t~r

- put coins/counters/pieces of paper slowly over words on the OHP screen and pupils spell them aloud before or as each is being masked;

- use stars in place of letters;
  e.g. (*un insecte: une a r * * g * é *)*

- use – instead of letters;
  e.g. *Bill a un po–s–on*

- show total number of letters;
  e.g. (*un animal: 6 lettres*) un o – – – – –

- show word on OHP upside down/back to front/mirror image;

- identify and spell words in a heap on OHP screen;

- show word with jumbled spelling.

There are doubtless many more which can be added to the list.

Adding an extra dimension

Adding an extra dimension means reinterpreting rather than starting from scratch. It is part of a planning stage. It does not involve rewriting but rather altering slightly activities in a coursebook. The purpose of this is to create cognitive conflict.

It's pairwork time. Pupils are working in twos: Partner A is trying to get directions from Partner B to find the location of various places in a town. Partner A has a map and a list of shops, places of entertainment, sports facilities and transport possibilities: Partner B has a detailed map, but with some recent building works and road closures marked on it. The language required by both partners has been extensively rehearsed before the pairwork began.

Are they all doing what you have set? Are they, without speaking a word of French, just showing each other the maps and cheating? You may not know for sure because to get round all the groups is not easy. So what can you do?

An answer might be to create an observer role. One pupil, chosen at random by the roll of a dice – lowest number is the observer – comments on and records what is said by the two pupils participating in the pairwork. This person can:

* seek clarification of either partner with questions like *'Tu peux répéter, s'il te plaît?'*;
* make a note of words/expressions that pupils in the pairwork did not know very well;
* ask the teacher to check vocabulary or spelling which they have heard but are not sure about. Example: observer to teacher: *'Ça s'écrit comment, pâtisserie?'*;
* even evaluate (sometimes) how a group is working; *'Bon travail'*, *'Génial!'*, *'Bonne prononciation!'* and other comments taken from familiar phrases modelled and used by the teacher can be part of the observer's evaluative repertoire. When this is done someone else can be the observer.

The advantages of this strategy are that criteria for assessment are agreed by all the class; nobody is excluded from the activity; the teacher is there to support where needed; the activity has an audience at all times.

key points	• We need to think through the purpose of the questions we ask.
	• Questions which focus on pupils' understanding of concepts can push them to think more than those which focus on content.
	• Interacting with pupils as we write up examples can keep them on their toes.
	• Copying from the board can be reinvented as a challenging activity for all.

Thinking about what learning a foreign language is all about

☐ How well do we listen to our learners?

☐ What do we listen for – information or accuracy?

☐ How important is a consideration of audience for the spoken or written word?

☐ What can we do to encourage learners to use language for their own purposes in a creative way?

chapter 4

To promote the idea that learning a language is about real communicative language use rather than rehearsal of that which has been learned by rote, listeners or readers should be encouraged to react to **what** is said rather than **how** it is said. Questions like: *Tu as des frères et des sœurs?* are normally answered by pupils with honest information which might be *J'ai un frère et une sœur*, to which an all-too-frequent response is *Excellent!* However, we need to stop and think about what message the word *Excellent!* (or *Super!* or *Bravo!*) is conveying. Is it excellent that:

a the pupil made a contribution to the lesson?
b the gender of the two indefinite articles, *un* and *une*, was correct?
c the parents stopped having children after the third one was born?!

Excellent! may not be appropriate because, in most situations, what we want to signal to our learners is that what they are saying, sometimes with a great effort to communicate, means something to us and is part of a genuine communicative event where the message matters. We should, as often as possible, interact with what is being said and reply perhaps:

Teacher *Tiens! Je ne savais pas. Il s'appelle comment, ton frère?*
Pupil *Fred.*
Teacher *Ah, Fred. Quel âge a-t-il, Fred?* etc

Often the words of praise that we use tend to signal that our interest is in the **grammatical accuracy** of the answer. If this is really what we want – which at times we certainly do – then other questions need to be asked and different responses made: a focus on form needs to kept distinct from a focus on content. If we do this then learners come to realise that the foreign language can be used to communicate real information, feelings, etc as well as that it needs to be accurate to avoid misunderstandings, ambiguity, etc.

Here is another example from a Year 5 class where the emphasis was on oral exchanges within the context of family. The class had already learnt the French alphabet and how to use the possessive adjectives, *mon, ma, mes, ton, ta, tes.*

Teacher *Comment s'appelle ton oncle, John?*
John *Il s'appelle Darion.*

Teacher   *Darion? Comment ça s'écrit?*
John   *D A R I O N.*

The student-teacher in this instance had not heard this name before, so, appropriately, signalled interest by asking how the name was spelt. The pupil was very pleased to answer because he knew the teacher was interested!

These two examples exemplify two key elements in authentic oral exchanges; there is an awareness of **audience** and a real **purpose** in the communication. The learners are being creative. What follows is an exploration of the idea of creativity which we believe is essential because to achieve it, 'it makes you think'.

Creativity: making language use your own

Based on the two key ideas of audience and purpose, where there is a clearly identified listener and/or reader, and a real reason to communicate, creativity is for the **learner**:

1 **Exploring** ways, which may be **linguistically original**, for creating meaning;
2 Discovering **new possibilities** in language already known; these may include **recombining** and putting into use, in **new contexts**, previously learned language.

These may be exemplified by learners:

3 Saying, writing, meeting words in combinations which may be **novel** to them;
4 **Experimenting** with language in order to convey a genuine message.

Creativity is for the **teacher**:

1 Encouraging learners to use language for **real communication** to a **genuine audience**;
2 Encouraging learners to explore the **world of the imagination**;
3 Encouraging learners to express their **own personal ideas, wishes, thoughts, interests**;
4 Devising activities which allow for **individual involvement** and **interpretation**.

A How to promote creative language use

There are several ways open to us. We can:

1   Make it a **deliberate, identified step** in a sequence of learning, for example:

- Start with a brainstorm by the learners of the target language they think is needed for a specific task before they imitate and repeat any new language. The teacher then presents the new language as he or she would normally with pictures, flashcards, etc;
- Add an unpredictable element – like the spelling request mentioned above, or a question like *'Tu es certain?'*. The teacher then explores as normal the grammar of what is being taught;
- Follow this with a request to use known language in a new context or to use it in a new medium, e.g. make a rhyme, rap, verse, poem, etc.

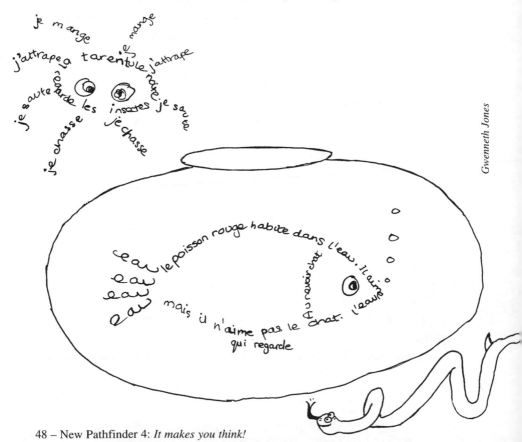

Gwenneth Jones

2   Model and encourage its use at **any time**, for example:

- As the feeling/need occurs, **saying** something;
- **Reading** just for fun/out of interest;
- **Writing** a message as the need arises.

3   Develop **classroom language** and **classroom instructions**, for example:

- Keep a record;
- Add words and expressions as they occur;
- Develop linguistic complexity.

The language **may** come from the learners' own language store and should be **repeatedly modelled** so that it is produced naturally. This process needs to be started at the earliest age, as we have suggested.

B The characteristics of creative activities

Creative activities often have:

1   a strong **individual** and **personal** focus;

2   an element of **personal choice** in terms of:

- subject matter
- interpretation
- degree of involvement.

C What teachers can do

The teacher can encourage:

- predicting content;
- personal reactions;
- fun and fantasy;
- use of the imagination;
- playing with words.

Examples:

- Re-combine known language in **original ways**:
  - manipulating words in a sentence;
  - changing sentences in a paragraph and seeing what happens.

- Use known language in new **settings**:
  - writing a poem, song.

- Include a variety of **emotional states**:
  - in pairwork;
  - in classwork dialogues.

EMOTIONS for use in pairwork

This illustration shows the wording on a collection of cards. The sheets will need to be photocopied and cut into separate cards for the game to be played.

How to use

The teacher gives out one card to each partner during pairwork. It is important that these are distributed **after** the language has been thoroughly practised in pairs in a normal way. Neither learner should see what the other card says. Each partner then re-enacts the dialogue/role play in a way which reflects the emotional state shown.

This photocopiable illustration can also be made into an overhead slide. When pairs of learners perform their dialogue/role play to the rest of the group, referring to the projected list of emotions, members of the class can work out which emotional state each of the partners is performing.

wütend	ungeduldig
faul	**ZUFRIEDEN**
gut gelaunt	*gestresst*
beunruhigt	unfreundlich

nett	höflich
unhöflich	unglücklich
traurig	

Encourage:

- Reading and listening to subject matter which is:
  - interesting to the pupil;
  - worth spending time on and which gives **pupils choice.**

  Examples:

  - magazines from target-language country;
  - reading (with or without recording);
  - what they do in class, in a joint project, homework tasks.

Encourage:

- Learners' **ideas and suggestions;**
- **Joint projects** with different contributors for known audiences.

  Examples:

- imaginary beasts	- bulletin board
- my ideal town	- recording, e-mail, fax
- small ads	- class magazine.
- posters	

D Why should we encourage a creative use of language?

1 It encourages a feeling of **purposeful** language use, rather than repeated practice, since it assumes an interested listener/reader/audience.
2 **Playing with words** and exploring the world of the imagination and emotions makes language use **personal**.
3 Personal use of language, in speaking and writing, reading and listening, **involves the learners as themselves**.
4 Creative language use promotes **language acquisition**.

To do and realise all of these learners have to **think**!

key points	• Language learning is about real communication, not just a rehearsal of phrases learned by rote.
	• Developing creativity means finding ways of getting pupils to make language work for their own purposes.
	• An audience and a clear purpose is needed for creative work.
	• Playing with words demands thought.

Talking about learning – the plenary phase

☐ How do we know that pupils understand what we teach?

☐ How can we encourage pupils to talk about what they have learnt?

☐ What might a plenary in MFL look like?

chapter 5

In answer to the question 'What did you learn?' pupils in language lessons, in our experience, focus almost exclusively on the **activities** they do, be that role play, filling in worksheets, learning new words with flashcards. It is rare that we find pupils who can articulate what it is they actually **learn** and how the activities they do support them in that endeavour. This is plainly not because they do not learn but because they are not used to talking about their learning. This articulation of learning requires thought and demands that they become cognisant of what it is to learn a language. This thought process – learning how to talk about learning (metacognition) – can help in cementing the learning. To extend the metaphor, metacognition can act as the mortar between the bricks of new knowledge. Understanding **how** they are learning heightens pupils' engagement since they can see that it is possible to improve and that it is possible to help themselves – there is no need to be completely in the thrall of the teacher.

Our colleague Barbro Carlsson in Mariesburg school in Karlstad, Sweden frequently gives learning homeworks. She routinely asks the class each to choose the words from the lesson's text that they will learn. Her key question for the group is 'How do you know you know a word?' This prompts a routine response from the class, ' You can say it. You can spell it. You can translate it. You can use it in a sentence'. Pupils then test each other on their learnt homework using the formula she has set up for proof of knowledge: they ask their partner to spell, translate, say or use in a sentence the words they have learnt. (2001)

We offer this example to suggest that getting pupils to think about the process of learning is not a giant leap into a new methodology but the Socratic principle: never explain until pupils understand.

In order to find out whether pupils understand we need to give them occasion to talk. It is far more challenging and effective and informative to get pupils to tell you what they have learnt from a lesson or activity than for you to tell them. For one thing we do not know is what it is that goes on in people's heads as they sit in front of us in the classroom. We may know what we meant to teach but it's the pupils who do the learning – this is the unpredictable nature of life in the classroom. It makes sense then that we create opportunities for them to tell us what they have learnt, since this, again, is an intellectually demanding activity.

> *Pupils' common experience of classrooms is that they just give truncated answers to questions. One figure for the average pupil contribution to whole-class discussion in Britain and the USA is under two seconds. The thinking behind such responses is floppy and half-formed. Being asked to clarify, extend and justify answers brings an edge to pupils' thinking.*
>
> (McGrane and Leat 2002: 1)

Getting pupils to think, offering them challenge, is the main focus of this book, so let's now concentrate on talking about learning with pupils. This process need not be onerous nor should it be too time-consuming.

You may be familiar with the term 'plenary' for this aspect of a lesson introduced into English schools by the National Literacy Strategy and the Key Stage 3 Strategy. The term means pulling together the threads of an activity or lesson and getting pupils to see where they are heading and where they have come from – in other words making connections for them which they may or may not have made for themselves. In a sense this is finding more sophisticated ways of asking the question which many MFL teachers ask at the end of a lesson, 'So what do you know now that you didn't know at the beginning of the lesson?' To this kind of question we suggest adding '... how do you know?' and '... how did you get there?'

Pupils in your school may well be familiar with a lesson structure which involves a lively beginning (a starter) and finishing with a 'plenary'. As mentioned above, such terminology has gained parlance in England in government-backed continuing professional development (CPD) initiatives. This can cause problems for teachers since these practices can quickly become humdrum for pupils if over-used. And herein lies our problem. We need to beware of the Record of Achievement scenario in which an essentially useful device lost credence with many pupils because of the repetitive and mechanistic nature of the exercise. The purpose was lost when pupils found themselves filling in records of achievement lesson after lesson as different departments required them to complete their records at the end of the term or year. It is essential that pupils don't become contemptuous of our attempts to make them more efficient and effective learners. Drawing the threads together should demonstrate that it's not just about thinking being shared but that new ideas and thoughts emerge from the process.

We feel that there is much to be gained in developing lesson routines which make pupils critically evaluate their own learning **and that of their peers** and identify ways to improve their learning and performance. But it is important to give it an MFL flavour and integrate it into teaching and learning so that they see the value of the process. The problem with multi-disciplinary CPD is that it is up to the subject teachers to interpret generic ideas to fit their own discipline.

The whole idea of developing metacognition through MFL is problematic. There is a perceived sophistication possible in other subjects which are principally taught through the medium of English while MFL teachers face the task of finding ways of conducting plenaries, for example, in the target language. Talking about what has been learnt could at first sight appear particularly difficult in the MFL classroom due to this tension between the place of English and the target language. But is it any more difficult than in other subject cultures? Pupils' response even to open questions may be very short and not get to any in-depth statement about what has been learnt. So we should teach pupils the language they need to talk about their learning, be that English or another language. Essentially, as teachers, we should consider when the talk is in the target language. We also might ask whether talking about it always moves the learning forward or underpins it.

So what might a plenary session look like in MFL?

In the examples below, the references refer to the MFL Teaching Objectives from the *Key Stage 3 Framework for MFL*. Readers teaching in England may find this useful for planning purposes.

Key purpose 1: Checking the rationale – why did we just do that?

Identify which is a statement and which is a question from a series of utterances by a Foreign Language Assistant. Discuss with the class the linguistic features or sound patterns which signalled the right decision. You might ask: How did you know that X was a question? Why is it important to know the difference?

Key purpose 2: Checking the process – how did you get there?

1   Challenge pupils to work in pairs and produce three sentences in which the word order in the target language is in contrast to word order in English. Ask them to explain the differences. (7S1, 9S1)

2   Provide a list of statements on OHT. By use of intonation pupils can be challenged to 'double your language'. The list of statements becomes a list of questions so long as the intonation is correct. Can pupils formulate simple questions from the list of statements? This could be a timed individual/pairwork challenge. You could begin a display list of ways to ask questions which could be referred to whenever relevant to the topic you are teaching.

Here is an example using PowerPoint so that the statement can be presented giving pupils time to think about the intonation of the question before the question itself is revealed. (Thanks to Philippe Rocca and Sylvie Urbistondoy, trainees on the CILT Graduate Teacher Programme.)

Double your French

- Carl est absent
- Madame X est prof d'anglais
- Il fait beau
- Aujourd'hui nous allons faire ...
- Tu as fini
- Vous êtes intelligents
- Tu es fou
- Jeudi, c'est ton anniversaire

- *Carl est absent?*
- *Madame X est prof d'anglais?*
- *Il fait beau?*
- *Aujourd'hui nous allons faire ...?*
- *Tu as fini?*
- *Vous êtes intelligents?*
- *Tu es fou?*
- *Jeudi, c'est ton anniversaire?*

Key purpose 3: Checking effectiveness – what helped you learn most effectively?

1 Show two sentences on an OHT, for example: '*J'aime le fromage. J'adore les bonbons*'. Challenge pupils to link them together using a connective. Collect a list of connectives and add them to a permanent list by the side of the board as they arise. (See p28: *Expand your answer* for an example in French to start you off.) Discuss the effect the use of the connectives has on the ideas they are able to express. (8W2, 8S2)

2 Pupils swap exercise books following written work and try to find (five) errors in their partner's work. They should have a reason for saying something is wrong.

Key purpose 4: Checking transference – what's the connection?

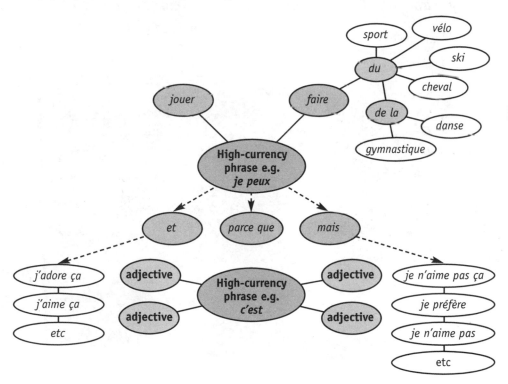

Conduct a brainstorm of the language covered during the topic you are teaching. Ask pupils in pairs to think of other contexts in which some of this language could be used. Above is an example of a 'mind map' which Curon Evans from Ysgol Glantaf constructed with his Year 8 pupils. It shows pupils that language is an organic entity. At the end of a topic he puts a 'high-currency' phrase in the middle of the board and asks pupils in pairs to add as much as they can to it. You can see here that they have mapped a series of sentences using the phrase *je peux* + infinitive. He keeps these maps, resurrecting them from time to time to get the class to add to them. In this way they become aware of the power and versatility of the language they are learning. You can see too the usefulness of such a device were it to form part of a display which grows lesson on lesson as pupils make more and more connections. This activity would lend itself well to some applications on interactive whiteboards. (8S3)

Key purpose 5: Checking understanding – what do you now know?

1 Magic board

You can see in the picture above a series of unsealed coloured envelopes stuck onto a board. You simply scribble on separate pieces of paper questions either in English or in the target language pertinent to the lesson and put one in each envelope. A volunteer is asked to choose an envelope by describing it, for example, *'L'enveloppe bleue à côté de l'enveloppe rose'*. Another pupil takes the slip of paper from the envelope and puts the question to the volunteer. The aim is for the class to open as many envelopes as possible before the signal for the end of the lesson. (Thanks to Coundon Court School and Technology College MFL department.)

2 All pupils have 'traffic lights' – red, and green, cards. They show a card to indicate their understanding – red = not understood. The teacher then chooses a pupil showing a green card to explain to the class what he or she has understood. Other green card holders can chip in if need be. If there are no green cards shown and you have run out of time then suggest that you'll go over the point in the next lesson.

3 'Snowball': pupils tell their partner three things they have learned this lesson/think of three questions they want to ask/make three sentences using the verbs you have looked at today, etc; they then join up with another pair and put their ideas together. Take two or three points of feedback from each group.

4 'Hot seat': an individual or group is put in the 'hot seat' and asked questions arising from the lesson and/or previous lessons. The rest of the group, in pairs initially, has to think up questions to put to this person in the target language and then ask him or her. (8S4)

Getting pupils to think and articulate their understanding is not easy in MFL. Teachers need to work collaboratively to create, clarify and consolidate their ideas. This discussion sheet, adapted from one devised by Susan Brearley from South Gloucester LEA, may be a useful starting point at a departmental meeting to get you talking and thinking. Consider ideas you and your colleagues have used for plenaries. Write these in the left-hand column (we have included some ideas to get you started). The chart is useful in getting you to think of the purpose of the plenary and to consider those classes for which the ideas are suitable.

Developing plenaries

Strategy	Currently in use Y/N	Advantages
Nominated pupil/pair summarises lesson, takes questions/feedback and invites answers from the rest of the class. Teacher input only as facilitator or 'expert'.		
All pupils have 'traffic lights' – red, and green, cards. They show a card to indicate their understanding – red = not understood; green = clearly understood.		
'Snowball' – tell your partner 3 things you have learned this lesson/think of 3 questions you want to ask/ make 3 sentences using the verbs you have looked at today, etc, then join up with another pair and put ideas together. Take 2/3 points of feedback from each group		
'Hot seat' – an individual or group is put in the 'hot seat' and the rest of the group have to agree questions about the lesson and then ask them.		

Disadvantages	Possible lessons/classes to experiment with

Other points when considering how to get pupils thinking through the use of plenaries

Pupils need to learn to ask the questions.

Observing how groups and pairs work is important. You need to create an opportunity to do this – taking mental notes or real notes of how groups are working or of particularly noteworthy contributions or use of target language (adhesive notes can be useful for making discreet notes for yourself and sticking them on the side of the board as you fill them. At the end of the lesson you can go back to them and feed back to the class 'X came up with this very good question earlier ...', 'X's pronunciation was excellent'.

Pupils need time to think.

Don't always evaluate the response yourself – set up an observer (*'type sympa'*) for pairs and small groups. Ask other pupils to comment – offer the ideas to the rest of the class.

If it is your practice to write lesson objectives on the board then refer back to them as each is achieved or in a plenary phase. Give pupils time to revise silently the key points of the lesson looking at the objectives. Follow with quick oral feedback.

key points	• **Pupils need to be taught how to articulate what they have learned and given the opportunity to do so.**
	• **Understanding how they have learnt something heightens pupils' engagement.**
	• **Pulling the threads of learning together in a plenary makes transparent the progress pupils are making.**
	• **It is useful for colleagues within the same department to work together to construct a bank of ideas for plenaries.**

Conclusion

During our years as teacher trainers and teachers we have come to perceive that there are techniques and practices that are common in MFL classrooms across the country; common activities we set up; common syllabuses we follow; common types of resources we use. In this book we have looked in detail at some of these common practices and asked stark questions about their purpose in terms of language learning and about whether they work as effective devices to encourage learning. It seems to us that it is useful at this time to go back to such basic principles since colleagues across the UK are suffering a crisis of pupil demotivation in languages. In order to do something about this we need to ask ourselves why this has been happening and significantly whether there is anything we can do about it. We decided that simply reinvigorating some of what we already do could go a long way in the fight to keep pupils interested in our subject. If we do not offer cognitive challenge, if we do not demand thought from pupils, then they are unlikely to take MFL seriously. We consider that offering challenge to pupils is partly about having the courage to ask ourselves the key question, 'Does this make them think?' rather than accepting off-the-shelf solutions which sometimes fall short of this. We are under pressure of time, without doubt, but can we afford not to ask ourselves this question?

> *Certainly the greatest enemy of understanding is coverage – the compulsion to touch on everything in the textbook or the syllabus just because it is there, rather than taking the time to present materials from multiple perspectives, allowing students to approach the materials in ways that are congenial to them but that ultimately challenge them.*

(Gardner and Boix-Mansilla 1999: 82)

Teaching is not about coverage but more about making connections for pupils. If pupils are not thinking in our lessons then, rest assured, we are not teaching what we think we are teaching.

Appendix: Ideas for a lively start to MFL lessons

References refer to the Teaching Objectives of the *Key Stage 3 Framework for MFL*, England (DfES 2003).

1   Four letters on the board: pupils find a word that fits under each letter (linked to a topic written at the top of the board). Pupils write these on mini-whiteboards and hold them up as they find words for you to approve or not. If they finish, they find another four words and see how many fours they can find before the formal beginning of the lesson. (This could involve use of a dictionary.) 7W1; 7W3

2   Envelopes on desks containing cut-up sentences to be put into order, or nouns to be put in gender columns, etc. 7W4; 7S2; 7S6; 8S1; 8S2

3   On mini-whiteboards which are on desks as pupils arrive, pupils write four words or sentences in the foreign language, one of which is an odd one out. They give their puzzle to another pupil to find the odd word out. 7W3; 7S3

4   On mini-whiteboards or paper pupils have to write eight words with a particular accent or feature (such as a double letter). See Pathfinder 33: *Stimulating grammatical awareness* (Rendall 1998) for similar ideas. 7W1; 7W3; 7W6

5   Each table has a part of a verb on a card on the desk. Pupils pick up their card and circulate. The object is to find three people with parts of the same verb. The group of four explains the link between the words. 7W5

6   Each table has a beginning or end of a sentence. Pupils circulate and must find a corresponding beginning or end. Those pupils sit together for the lesson and the first activity is to make up a new end to the sentence. 7S6; 7T5

7   Find a paragraph per fortnight of a current news item (try **www.euronews.com** or **www.bbc.co.uk/worldservice/us/languages.shtml** where you will find news in a wide variety of languages). They underline in red those words they know, in blue those words they can guess and in black those words they definitely don't know. After a given time, as a class, they tell the teacher the gist of the news article. 7T3; 8T1; 9T3

8   Write a text which is full of mistakes on an OHT or a poster. Pupils must list the mistakes they spot on their mini-whiteboards or correct a paper version. Show them a corrected version so that they can see how many mistakes they have found. This should be a quick activity and so the text may be short. The incorrect text shouldn't remain on view for long in order to avoid pupils remembering the mistakes rather than the corrections. 8W4; 7W4

9   Pupils have to memorise five new key words for the lesson which are on the board as they come in – full 'memorisation' will mean they can say it/spell it/translate it/use it in a sentence. These could be recorded in vocabulary books. 7W7; 9W7

10 At the beginning of a new topic, the topic title appears on the board. Pupils in pairs draw a 'mind map' on paper or mini-whiteboards of all of the words or phrases in the target language they can make from their prior knowledge. This will lead into a whole-class brainstorming session in preparation for this topic. 7S3; (8S3); 8T1

11 Draw a picture of two mouths on the board with a set of ten teeth. One labelled *Prof./Lehrer(in)/Professor,* the other *Elèves/Schüler/Estudiente.* The purpose of the game is competition again the teacher. For every question/word, etc, the class get right the teacher loses a tooth and for every one the class get wrong they lose a tooth. Or you can have two teams playing against each other with a mouth each. 7S4; 8S4

12 Write three words/sentences on the board which the class will chant. Someone leaves the room. The class decides who will be the *chef d'orchestre* and a sign which will signal a change of chant (e.g. *chef* scratching left ear). Pupil re-enters the room. Class chant the first word/sentence until the *chef* makes the sign very

discreetly so that it is not clear who is leading the chant. When they see the *chef* make the sign the class move on to chanting word/phrase number two. The object of the game is for the chosen pupil to discover who the *chef d'orchestre* is.

13 Pronouns with verbs are written on the board – mixed up. Pupils come to the board and draw a line joining the correct pronoun with a correct form of a verb. The rest of the class say, *'vrai'* or *'faux'/'richtig'* or *'falsch/'verdad'* or *'falso'*. 7W5; 9W6

14 Work on sounds of the language, especially those which are more difficult (vowels, nasal sounds in French). Class write on mini-whiteboards the words they know which contain a particular sound. Pool these on the board once pupils have had time to think. 7W7; 7W6

15 Each pair in the class has a whiteboard. You (or a pupil) give, in the target language, a collective noun, e.g. shops. Each pair has to write a word/sentence in the target language incorporating a word in this category, e.g. supermarket. 7W3

16 Ask a question and throw the ball to a pupil. The pupil who catches the ball has to answer the question, ask another question and throw the ball to another pupil who answers the question and asks another question and throws the ball, etc. In Year 7 they are allowed to repeat questions so long as it's not directly following on from the last. 7S4

17 Pupils pass around a bag of plastic letters to music. When the music stops, the pupil holding the bag must select a letter and call it aloud to the class in the target language. The first person to make a word from the accumulated letters wins. 7W1; 7W3

18 Read a list of ten to twelve items of vocabulary slowly and then repeat the list. Pupils must not write anything while you read the list. Then pupils are challenged to write ten words from the list and the first to do so wins a point. 7W1; 7W3

19 Display list of nouns (without article) on the board/OHP. Pupils have to categorise into masculine/feminine/neuter. 8W4

20 Reveal a word on the OHP. Pupils compete to see who can write a sentence including the word in the shortest time. 7S1; 8S1

21 Ask a pupil to select a piece of paper from an envelope. The pupil reads the word/phrase to the class. Pupils compete to see who can be the first to write a sentence/two sentences including this word or phrase on their mini-whiteboards. 7S9

22 Display answers to questions, for which pupils must provide the questions. 7S4; 8S4

23 Write a simple statement on the board/OHP, e.g. *J'aime l'anglais.* Pupils are challenged to extend the sentence to a minimum of ten words, e.g. *J'aime l'anglais parce que le prof est très sympa, mais je déteste la géo parce que c'est vraiment compliqué.* 7S6; 8S2; 9S6

24 The teacher writes a word on the board, e.g. *'aime'*. Pupils are challenged to write a sentence including the key word with at least ten words in it. 7S6; 8S2; 9S6

25 OHP memory game. The teacher displays a picture on the OHP, e.g. the interior of a flat (colour should be used). Pupils have five minutes to work in pairs to recall in the target language fifteen facts about the image they have just seen. 7S6; 9S6

26 Choose two key phrases for the lesson for pupils to understand and actively use by the end of the lesson. These will be about classroom management rather than part of the content of the lesson (e.g. it's my turn, it's your turn). Demonstrate their usage, then challenge pupils to use these expressions whenever they can in the lesson. Each time you hear the expressions used in the correct context you award a point. 7S9

27 Pupils study a paragraph on the OHP for a given time. The text is removed. Pupils try to recall and note down twenty words they have just seen in the text. This works well in pairs. 7W7

(Our thanks to teachers on the Crawley and Exeter CILT two-day Key Stage 3 courses and to Rachel Redfearn of Wakefield LEA for their ideas and inspiration.)

References

Department for Education and Skills (2003) *Key Stage 3 National Strategy. Framework for teaching Modern Foreign Languages: Years 7, 8 and 9.* HMSO.

Gardner, H. and Boix-Mansilla, V. (1999) 'Teaching for understanding in the disciplines – and beyond'. In: Leach, J. and Moon, B. (eds) *Learners and pedagogy.* Open University Press.

Harris, V., Burch, J., Jones, B. and Darcy, J. (2001) *Something to say? Promoting spontaneous classroom talk.* CILT.

McGrane, J. and Leat, D. (2002) 'Developing debriefing skills: The gateway to metacognition and transfer'. In *Topic,* Spring 2002 Issue 27.

The Open University (2001) *Iliad CD-ROM.* The Open University.

Rendall, H. (1998) Pathfinder 33: *Stimulating grammatical awareness: A fresh look at language acquisition.* CILT.

Further reading

Alison, J. and Halliwell, S. (2002) Classic Pathfinder 2: *Challenging classes: Focus on pupil behaviour.* CILT.

Harris, V. and Snow, D. (2004) Classic Pathfinder 4: *Doing it for themselves: Focus on learning strategies and vocabulary building.* CILT.

Jones, B. and Jones, G. (2001) *Boys' performance in Modern Foreign Languages: Listening to learners.* CILT.

Jones, B., Halliwell, S. and Holmes, B. (2002) Classic Pathfinder 1: *You speak, they speak: Focus on target language use.* CILT.

McLachlan, A. (2002) New Pathfinder 1: *Raising the standard: Addressing the needs of gifted and talented pupils.* CILT.

Swarbrick, A. (2002) *Aspects of teaching secondary Modern Foreign Languages.* RoutledgeFalmer.

UNIVERSITY OF WALES
CYNCOED